365
Appleseeds

A Grateful Gift for Teachers

by Kathy Wagoner

SOURCEBOOKS, INC.®
NAPERVILLE, ILLINOIS

Published by Sourcebooks, Inc.
P.O. Box 4410, Naperville, Illinois 60567-4410
(630) 961-3900
FAX: (630) 961-2168

ISBN 1-57071-700-1

Printed and bound in the United States of America

DR   10   9   8   7   6   5   4   3   2   1

In one way or another, each of us is a teacher. A few people, however, devote their lives to this noble profession. They share of themselves so that others may grow and learn. This book provides thanks and encouragement to those teachers in our lives.

A teacher affects eternity; no one can tell where his influence stops.

—Henry Adams

The potential of a child is the most intriguing and stimulating thing in all creation.

—Ray L. Wilbur

The long journey toward
the end of the chapter
begins with a short step
into that first paragraph.

It is in identifying yourself
with the hopes,
dreams, fears and
longings of others that you may
understand them and help them.

-Wilfred A. Peterson

What we hope ever
to do with ease,
we must learn first to do
with diligence.

-Samuel johnson

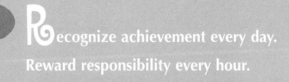

Recognize achievement every day.
Reward responsibility every hour.

Education has for its object
the formation of character.

—Herbert Spencer

Experience is the name that everyone gives to his mistakes.

—Oscar Wilde

Every person is gifted in some area. We just have to find out what.

—Evelyn Blose Holman

9

Listening is the shortest distance between two people.

The man who does not read good books has no advantage over the man who cannot read them.

-Mark Twain

If you always do what you always did,
you'll always get what you always got.

—Verne Hill

I touch the future. I teach.

—Christa McAuliffe

He who praises everybody
praises nobody.

—Samuel Johnson

Lucky is the teacher whose students want to know how things work.

Reading maketh
a full man, conference a
ready man, and writing an
exact man.

-Francis Bacon

Nothing is so strong
as gentleness;
nothing so gentle as real
strength.

–St. Francis de Sales

Training means learning the rules.
Experience means learning the
exceptions.

Maturing is the process by which the individual becomes conscious of the equal importance of each of his fellow men.

—Alvin Goeser

That I may care enough to love enough to share enough to let others become what they can be.

—John O'Brien

What sculpture is to a
block of marble, education
is to a human soul.

—Joseph Addison

The cost of educating

22 a child today is immense. But

the cost of not educating a

child is incalculable.

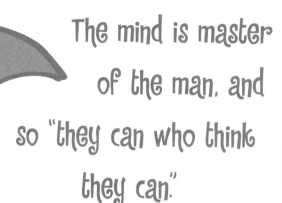

The mind is master
of the man, and
so "they can who think
they can."

-Nixon Waterman

A book should teach us to enjoy life, or to endure it.

—Samuel Johnson

The scholar who cherishes
the love of comfort is not fit to
be deemed a scholar.

—Confucius

just think of the tragedy of teaching children not to doubt.

—Clarence Darrow

The mind can absorb only
what the seat can endure.

Children are our most
valuable natural resource.

-Herbert Hoover

28

Every great man is
always being helped
by everybody; for
his gift is to get good out
of all things and all persons.

-John Ruskin

If we were supposed to talk more than we listen, we would have two mouths and one ear.

—Mark Twain

I am not a teacher—only a fellow traveler of whom you asked the way. I pointed ahead—ahead of myself as well as of you.

—George Bernard Shaw

If at first you don't succeed, don't worry because neither did the teacher in the next classroom.

You must never tell
a thing. You must
illustrate it. We learn
through the eye and
not the noggin.

—Will Rogers

The right angle to solve a difficult problem is the "try-angle."

–Ellis I. Levitt

One of a student's biggest fears is not being listened to.

36

A master can tell you what he expects of you. A teacher, though, awakens your own expectations.

—Patricia Neal

The one exclusive sign of thorough knowledge is the power of teaching.

—Aristotle

An error of opinion may be tolerated
where reason is left free to combat it.

—Thomas Jefferson

If you make two people
in your classroom happy
today, be sure one of them
is you.

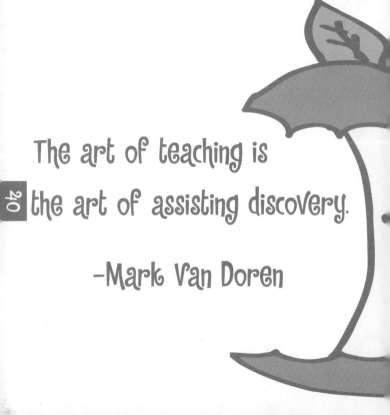

The art of teaching is
40 the art of assisting discovery.

-Mark Van Doren

A student who tries something and fails is better than a student who does nothing and succeeds.

Child, give me your hand that I may walk in the light of your faith in me.

—Hannah Kahn

Misinformation is one of the greatest dangers of modern education.

—Charles F. Kettering

Lucky is the teacher who can look across the room and not see one bored face.

The object of teaching a child is to enable him to get along without his teacher.

—Elbert Hubbard

Our greatest glory
consists not in
never falling, but in rising
every time we fall.

-Oliver Goldsmith

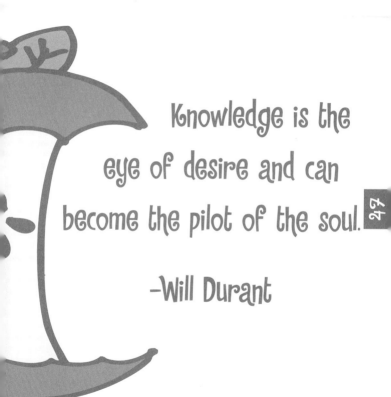

Knowledge is the
eye of desire and can
become the pilot of the soul. 47

-Will Durant

Men, in teaching others, learn themselves.

—Seneca

Be patient with your students. The rate may be slow, but the growth is immense!

They are ill discoverers that think there is no land, when they can see nothing but sea.

—Francis Bacon

Answer me in one word.

—William Shakespeare

Education is helping
the child realize his
potentialities.

-Erich Fromm

52

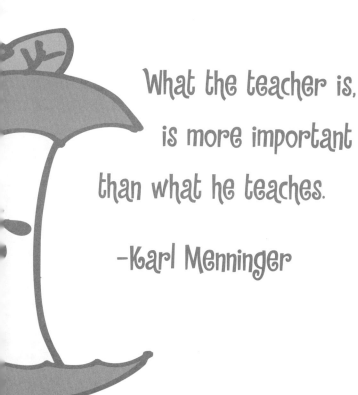

What the teacher is,
is more important
than what he teaches.

-Karl Menninger

53

The true aim of everyone who aspires to be a teacher should be, not to impart his own opinion, but to kindle minds.

A person who cannot read knows only what he is told.

Thinking is the hardest work there is.

—Henry Ford

Teaching for tests creates learnoids.

—Alan Scott Winston

The object of education is to prepare the young to educate themselves throughout their lives.

-Robert Maynard Hutchins

A chain is only as strong as its weakest link, and to limit teaching to the lowest level of understanding does not make the chain any stronger.

Teaching is fun.

—Jaime Escalante

Music training is a more potent instrument than any other, because rhythm and harmony find their way into the inward places of the soul.

—Plato

In teaching, it is the method and not the content that is the message…the drawing out, not the pumping in.

—Ashley Montagu

your students' successes
are ultimately your own.

A wise man's heart guides his mouth, and his lips promote instruction.

-Prov. 16:23 (NIV)

Everyone is ignorant,
only on different subjects. 65

-Will Rogers

Anytime you see a turtle up on top of a fence post, you know he had some help.

—Alex Haley

Expect your students to be winners. Expect your students to be the best.

He that revels in a well-chosen library
has innumerable dishes and all of
admirable flavor.

—William Godwin

We know what we are,
but not what we may be.

—William Shakespeare

Experience is the
child of thought and
thought is the child of action.

-Benjamin Disraeli

When you help someone up a hill, you're that much nearer the top yourself.

75

Train a child in a way he should go; and when he is old, he will not turn from it.

—Prov. 22:6 (NIV)

Don't let failure go to your head.

—Haim Ginott

The teacher is like a candle that lights others at the risk of consuming itself.

75

How the children
turn out will depend
on what we put into
the effort.

—Lottie Taylor

Blessed is the
influence of one true,
loving human soul on another.

-George Eliot

There is one thing stronger than all the armies in the world, and that is an idea whose time has come.

-Victor Hugo

Come what come may, Time
and the hour runs through the
roughest day.

Teachers make hope happen.

No student knows his subject. The most he knows is where and how to find out the things he does not know.

—Woodrow Wilson

Intelligence defies fate.
So long as a man can
think, he is free.

—Ralph Waldo Emerson

If a man empties his purse into his head, no man can take it from him. An investment in knowledge always pays the best interest.

-Benjamin Franklin

Knowledge comes,
but wisdom lingers.

-Alfred, Lord Tennyson

A man should learn to sail in all winds.

—Italian proverb

A teacher is one who, in his youth, admired teachers.

—H. L. Mencken

Patience is the ability to idle your motor when you feel like stripping your gears.

The teacher is one
who makes two ideas
grow where only one
grew before.

—Elbert Hubbard

We need to make
education a community
obsession.

-Joan Kowal

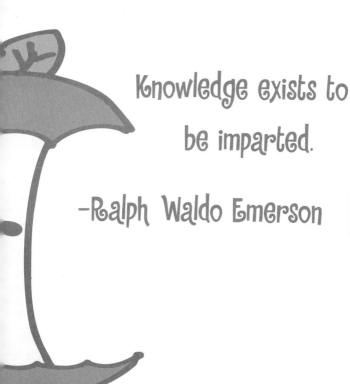

Knowledge exists to
be imparted.

-Ralph Waldo Emerson

93

Science is simply common sense at its best.

—T. H. Huxley

Education is what survives
when what has been learned
has been forgotten

—B. F. Skinner

The most complicated concept can be mastered by breaking it down into small parts.

You have to be either critically loving or a loving critic, but you should never be indifferent.

—John Gardner

Example is always
more efficacious
than precept.

-Samuel Johnson

I have the basic
belief that all children
can learn. Our expectation
is that they will.

-Carol Purvis

Better three hours too soon than a minute too late.

—William Shakespeare

He who wrestles with us strengthens our nerves and sharpens our skills.

—Edward Burke

Better to do a little well than a great deal poorly. Life's greatest adventure is in doing one's level best.

—Arthur Morgan

Education is the ticket to success.

—Jaime Escalante

To have inspired a student to become the person he wants to be is a teacher's greatest achievement.

We speak of educating our children. Do we know that our children educate us?

-Lydia Sigourney

Chaos often breeds life, where
order breeds but habit.

—Henry Adams

A good education teaches a student what to remember from the past, what to enjoy in the present, and what to plan for in the future.

The mediocre teacher tells. The good teacher explains. The superior teacher demonstrates. The great teacher inspires.

—William Arthur Ward

I teach with my heart
and my soul and not
with my mouth alone.

—Jaime Escalante

Wouldn't it be wonderful if people valued education as much as they value schooling?

Recognize differences.
Don't alter your
expectations, but alter
your approach.

-Annie Benford Duvall

107

For he that was only taught by himself had a fool for a master.

—Ben Jonson

Education is growth.

—John Dewey

An error is not a terror.

—Haim Ginott

$\mathbf{W}$e're here to help children succeed. It's that simple.

—Elaine Collins

The secret of education lies
in respecting the pupil.

-Ralph Waldo Emerson

In the garden of learning, the seeds that are planted today will produce tomorrow's harvest.

113

This will never be a civilized country until we spend more money for books than we do for chewing gum.

—Elbert Hubbard

Great works are performed not
by strength but by perseverance.

—Samuel Johnson

Be strong enough so that nothing can disturb your peace of mind...not even a paper airplane that sails across the back of the room while you are speaking.

Children have more need of models than of critics.

—Joseph Joubert

Difficult: that which can be done immediately. Impossible: that which takes a little longer.

-George Santayana

It is easier to
move a cemetery
than to effect a change in
curriculum.

-Woodrow Wilson

A child miseducated is a child lost.

—John F. Kennedy

I beg of you to stop apologizing
for being a member of the most
important profession in the world.

—William G. Carr

The president of the United States fifty years from now is sitting in a classroom, being taught, being inspired; and she is having a good day.

To accomplish great things, we must not only act but also dream, not only plan but also believe.

—Anatole France

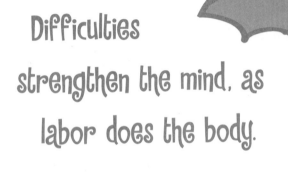

Difficulties
strengthen the mind, as
labor does the body.

-Seneca

A classroom full of students is like a team. Everyone needs to work together to win the game.

Learning is like rowing upstream—not to advance is to drop back.

—Chinese proverb

The man who can make hard
things easy is the educator.

—Ralph Waldo Emerson

Treat people as if they were what they ought to be, and you help them to become what they are capable of being.

—Johann Von Goethe

There is a destiny that makes us brothers; none goes his way alone: All that we send into the lives of others comes back into our own.

—Edwin Markham

I find that a great part of the information I have was acquired by looking up something else on the way.

-Franklin P. Adams

Even the gifted and talented student needs help, support, and encouragement to succeed.

Consider the postage stamp. Its usefulness consists in the ability to stick to one thing until it gets there.

—Josh Billings

Few things help an individual more than to place responsibility upon him, and to let him know that you trust him.

—Booker T. Washington

He that has patience may compass anything.

—François Rabelais

Natural abilities are
like natural plants; they
need pruning by study.

—Francis Bacon

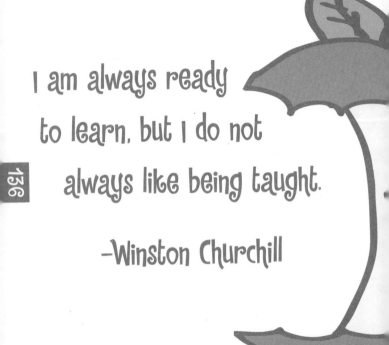

I am always ready
to learn, but I do not
always like being taught.

136

-Winston Churchill

Failing to prepare
is preparing to fail.

-Anonymous

137

More matter, with less art.

—William Shakespeare

Vast numbers of Americans rely as much on astrology as on astronomy. We have a way to go in education.

—Stephanie Pace Marshall

People who aren't in education just don't know what they're missing.

—Keith Blue

A minute's success pays
for the years of failure.

—Robert Browning

New knowledge grows from the seeds of what is already known.

Those who educate children
well are more to be
honored than even
their parents, for these only
give them life; those the art
of living well.

-Aristotle

After the verb "to love," "to help" is the most beautiful verb in the world.

—Bertha von Suttner

The hardest part about being a good teacher is that you have to do it every day.

That's what learning is. You suddenly understand something you've understood all your life, but in a new way.

—Doris Lessing

The system of classifying students as "special needs," "at risk," or "talented and gifted" fails to recognize that all students are unique.

By learning you
will teach, by teaching
you will learn.

-Latin proverb

It is greater work to educate a child, in the true and larger sense of the word, than to rule a state.

-William Ellery Channing

149

Our progress as a nation can
be no swifter than our progress
in education.

—John F. Kennedy

When a teacher really gets to know a student, a partnership is created that allows learning to be accomplished.

We teachers can only help the work going on, as servants wait upon a master.

—Maria Montessori

153

The foundation of every state is the education of its youth.

—Diogenes

'Tis education forms the common mind, just as the twig is bent, the tree's inclined.

-Alexander Pope

To teach is to learn twice.

-Joseph Joubert

Education is a better safeguard of liberty than a standing army.

—Edward Everett

Children have to be educated,
but they have also to be left to
educate themselves.

—Abbé Dimnet

Happy is he who has been able to learn the causes of things.

—Virgil

Knowledge is the
true organ of sight,
not the eyes.

—Panchatantra

Education is not the filling of a pail, but the lighting of a fire.

-William Butler Yeats

Teachers give all that they are able to persuade their students to take.

One looks back with appreciation to the brilliant teachers, but with gratitude to those who touched our human feelings.

—Carl Jung

Education is a wonderful thing. If you couldn't sign your name, you'd have to pay cash.

—Rita Mae Brown

Education is the best provision for old age.

—Aristotle

165

The end and aim of all education is the development of character.

—Francis W. Parker

It was my teacher's genius, her quick sympathy, her loving tact which made the first years of my education so beautiful.

-Helen Keller

Good teaching is
one-fourth preparation
and three-fourths theater.

–Gail Godwin

Education makes people easy to lead, but difficult to drive; easy to govern, but impossible to enslave.

—Henry Peter Brougham

If you are a teacher you can change the world because it's your world. You can have an influence on your sphere, your domain.

—Senator Barbara Mikulski

Surely, therefore, the very nature and needs of the contemporary world make the teacher an indispensable member of society.

—Calvin O. Davis

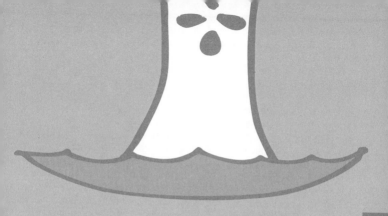

Education is freedom.

—André Gide

171

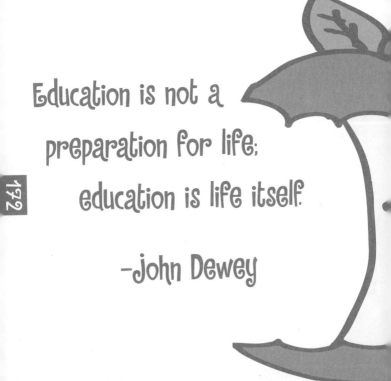

Education is not a
preparation for life;
education is life itself.

-John Dewey

174

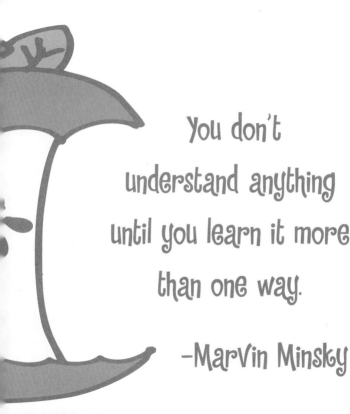

You don't
understand anything
until you learn it more
than one way.

-Marvin Minsky

Education is the taming of domestication of the soul's raw passions—not suppressing them or excising them, which would deprive the soul of its energy—but forming and informing them as art.

—Allan Bloom

Seeing a child's successful progress during the school year confirms a teacher's calling to the profession.

Education must have an end in view,
for it is not an end in itself.

—Sybil Marshall

It made me gladsome
to be getting some
education, it being like
a big window opening.

—Mary Webb

Memorizing facts
does little to teach how to
achieve desired results.

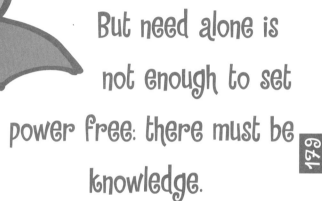

But need alone is
not enough to set
power free: there must be
knowledge.

-Ursula K. Le Guin

179

We have a hunger of the mind which asks for knowledge of all around us, and the more we gain, the more is our desire; the more we see, the more are we capable of seeing.

—Maria Mitchell

It is not only by the questions we have answered that progress may be measured, but also by those we are still asking. The passionate controversies of one era are viewed as sterile preoccupations by another, for knowledge alters what we seek as well as what we find.

—Freda Adler

Worlds can be found by a child and an adult bending down and looking together under the grass stems or at the skittering crabs in a tidal pool.

—Mary Catherine Bateson

Everything is data. But
data isn't everything.

—Pauline Bart

One can learn, at least. One can go on learning until the day one is cut off.

-Fay Weldon

The joy of learning
is as indispensable
in study as breathing is in
running.

-Simone Weil

185

The world of learning is so broad, and the human soul is so limited in power! We reach forth and strain every nerve, but we seize only a bit of the curtain that hides the infinite from us.

—Maria Mitchell

The excitement of learning separates youth from old age. As long as you're learning you're not old.

—Rosalyn S. Yalow

The way to do research is to attack the facts at the point of greatest astonishment.

—Celia Green

Teaching is the royal
road to learning.

—Jessamyn West

If you can keep your
head when all
about you are losing
theirs, it's just possible you
haven't grasped the situation.

-Jean Kerr

Using good grades as the measure of one's success in learning is meaningless if nothing is learned truly.

191

Knowledge advances by steps and not by leaps.

—Thomas Macaulay

Education is learning what you
didn't even know you didn't know.

—Daniel J. Boorstin

Education is the ability to listen to almost anything without losing your temper or your self-confidence.

—Robert Frost

Education should be a lifelong process, the formal period serving as a foundation on which life's structure may rest and rise.

—Robert H. Jackson

Intelligence plus character—that is the goal of true education.

—Martin Luther King, Jr.

Until the student knows how much you care, he won't care how much you know.

Education should consist of a series of enchantments, each raising the individual to a higher level of awareness, understanding, and kinship with all living things.

—Anonymous

To know how to suggest is the great art of teaching.

—Henri Amiel

Learn something new each day and prosper.

A teacher's major contribution may pop out anonymously in the life of some ex-student's grandchild.

—Wendell Berry

Come, give us a
taste of your quality.

-William Shakespeare

Teachers provide a social and intellectual environment in which students can learn.

-James MacGregor Burns

The true teacher does not teach, yet one may educate oneself at his side; in just the same way the wise man does not create folk culture, but it takes form naturally in his presence.

—Vinoba Bhave

The teacher who walks in the shadow of the temple, among his followers, gives not of his wisdom but rather of his faith and his lovingness. If he is indeed wise he does not bid you enter the house of his wisdom, but rather leads you to the threshold of your own mind.

—Kahlil Gibran

Learning is continuous, for to stop would be like reading yesterday's newspaper forever.

It is the supreme art of
the teacher to awaken joy
in creative expression
and knowledge.

—Albert Einstein

The greatest sign of success for a teacher..is to be able to say, "The children are now working as if I did not exist."

-Maria Montessori

When the student is ready, the teacher arrives; when the teacher is ready, the student arrives.

—Anonymous

Genius is one percent inspiration and ninety-nine percent perspiration.

—Thomas Alva Edison

Children learn to creep ere they can learn to go.

—John Heywood

Teach by doing whenever you can, and only fall back upon words when doing it is out of the question.

—Rousseau

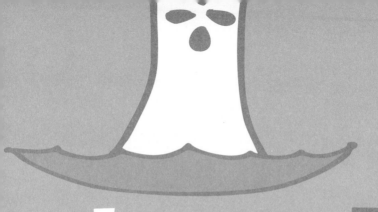

The educator is like a good gardener, whose function is to make available healthy, fertile soil in which a young plant can grow strong roots.

—E. F. Schumacher

A teacher who can unlock a student's potential has helped to make the world a better place.

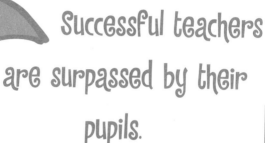

Successful teachers
are surpassed by their
pupils.

-Anonymous

Teachers open the door, but you must enter by yourself.

—Chinese proverb

A student's future occupation depends on his or her present education.

The boughs of no two trees ever have the same arrangement. Nature always produces individuals; she never produces classes.

—Lydia Maria Child

A student who learns
from failure will have
achieved success.

219

One must separate
from anything that
forces one to repeat "No"
again and again.

-Friedrich Nietzsche

The practice of "reviewing"...in general has nothing in common with the art of criticism.

-Henry James

222

Perfection is the child of Time.

—Bishop Joseph Hall

We never do anything well
till we cease to think about the
manner of doing it.

—William Hazlitt

The force of necessity is irresistible.

—Aeschylus

He who can't remember clearly his own childhood is a poor educator.

—Marie von Ebner-Eschenbach

Before beginning,
prepare carefully.

-Cicero

You may talk too much on the best of subjects.

–Benjamin Franklin

227

Readers are plentiful;
thinkers are rare.

—Harriet Martineau

My days ran away so fast. I simply ran after my days.

—Leah Morton

The responsibility a dedicated teacher feels for educating students is considerable indeed.

Those having torches will
pass them on to others.

—Plato

The true teacher
defends his pupils
against his own personal
influence.

-A. B. Alcott

The rule is, jam
tomorrow and
jam yesterday–but never
jam today.

–Lewis Carroll

233

I would help others, out of a fellow-feeling.

—Robert Burton

Establishing lasting peace is
the work of education.

—Maria Montessori

History repeats itself because learning from the past requires a longer memory than most possess.

Rome was not built
in one day.

—John Heywood

238

Woe be to him that
reads but one book.

-George Herbert

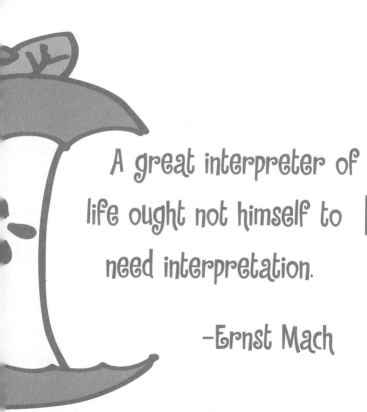

A great interpreter of life ought not himself to need interpretation.

-Ernst Mach

239

To know when one's self is interested, is the first condition of interesting other people.

—Walter Pater

The byproduct is sometimes more valuable than the product.

—Havelock Ellis

There is always one moment in childhood when the door opens and lets the future in.

—Graham Greene

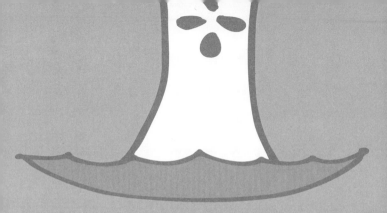

We shouldn't teach
great books; we should
teach a love of reading.

—B. F. Skinner

A teacher is one who understands that a concept can be voiced aloud, but until there is comprehension, there has been no true learning.

Mix a little foolishness with your serious plans: it's lovely to be silly at the right moment.

245

-Horace

If a little knowledge is dangerous,
where is the man who has so much
as to be out of danger?

—T. H. Huxley

The supreme achievement
is to accomplish that which
cannot be done.

You can cover a great deal of country in books.

—Andrew Lang

One does not know—
cannot know—the best
that is in one.

—Friedrich Nietzsche

There is no substitute
for hard work.

-Thomas Alva Edison

250

Tact is, after all, a kind of mind-reading.

251

-Sarah Orne Jewett

Learn, compare, collect the facts!

—Ivan Petrovich Pavlov

Only those ideas that are least truly ours can be adequately expressed in words.

—Henri Bergson

Experience, the universal Mother of Sciences.

—Miguel de Cervantes

No rule is so general,
which admits not some
exception.

—Robert Burton

Teaching someone how to think, not what to think, is easier said than done.

Hold their noses to grindstone.

-John Heywood

257

If you can look into the
seeds of time,
And say which grain will
grow and which will not,
Speak.

—William Shakespeare

How shall I be able to rule over others, that have not full power and command of myself?

—François Rabelais

Since I would rather make of him (the child) an able man than a learned man, I would also urge that care be taken to choose a (tutor) with a well-made rather than a well-filled head.

—Michel de Montaigne

If we would have new
knowledge, we must get
a world of new questions.

—Susan Langer

Look to the essence of
a thing, whether it
be a point of
doctrine, of practice, or of
interpretation.

-Marcus Aurelius Antoninus

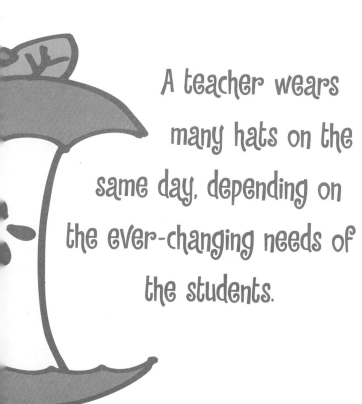

A teacher wears many hats on the same day, depending on the ever-changing needs of the students.

263

The chief merit of language is clearness, and we know that nothing detracts so much from this as do unfamiliar terms.

—Galen

All things are filled full of signs, and it is a wise man who can learn about one thing from another.

—Plotinus

Success and failure are intertwined. Babe Ruth led the league in strikeouts in the same year that he hit sixty home runs.

No one cares to speak to an unwilling listener. An arrow never lodges in a stone: often it recoils upon the sender of it.

—St. Jerome

Hear the other side.

-St. Augustine

268

He listens well who takes notes.

-Dante Alighieri

269

The more wise and powerful a master, the more directly is his work created, and the simpler it is.

—Meister Eckhart

Reflection at the end of the day provides perspective to begin again tomorrow.

Learning without thought is labor lost; thought without learning is perilous.

—Confucius

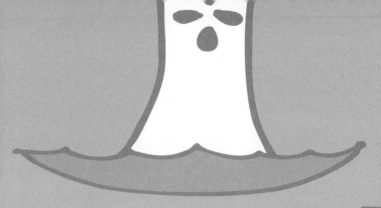

Much learning does
not teach understanding.

—Heraclitus

Let early education
be a sort of
amusement; you will
then be better able to find
out the natural bent.

-Plato

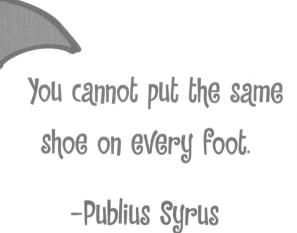

You cannot put the same
shoe on every foot.

-Publius Syrus

275

Nothing is so difficult but that it
may be found out by seeking.

—Terence (Publius Terentius Afer)

The very spring and root of honesty
and virtue lie in good education.

—Plutarch

A good mind possesses a kingdom.

—Seneca

The example set by others does more to teach values than many hours of lecture.

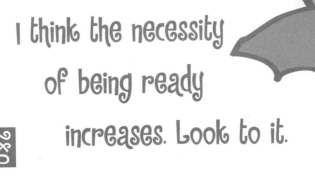

I think the necessity
of being ready
increases. Look to it.

-Abraham Lincoln

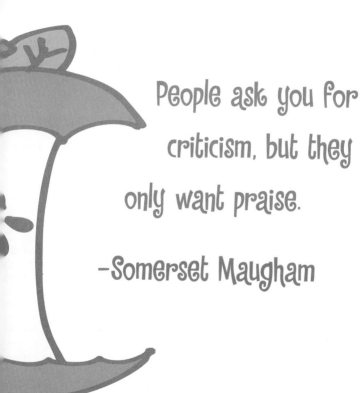

People ask you for
criticism, but they
only want praise.

281

-Somerset Maugham

The fate of the books depends on the capacity of the reader.

—Terentianus Maurus

In all things we learn only
from those we love.

—Johann Von Goethe

Teaching that would lay any claim at all to distinction, if not to actual greatness, is the influence of personality upon personality, rather than the mere imparting of a set of facts.

—Frank E. Gaebelein

Sometimes a person's mind
is stretched by a new idea
and never does go back to its
old dimensions.

—Oliver Wendell Holmes

A good example
can make the solution to a
complex problem clear.

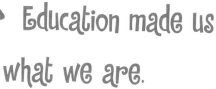

Education made us
what we are.

-Claude-Adrian Helvetius

Education is simply the soul of
a society as it passes from one
generation to another.

—G. K. Chesterton

A child can be saved from the worst circumstances by providing the opportunity for a good education.

I have learned since to be a better student, and to be ready to say to my fellow students, "I do not know."

—William Osler

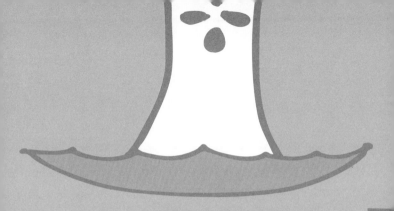

We class schools, you see,
into four grades: Leading School,
First-rate School, Good School,
and School.

—Evelyn Waugh

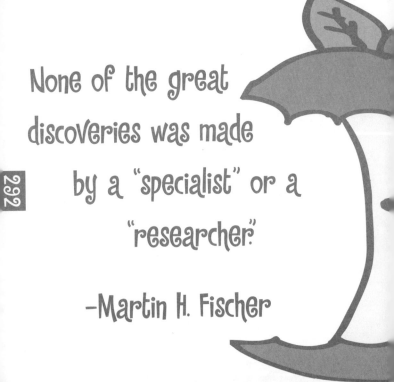

None of the great
discoveries was made
by a "specialist" or a
"researcher."

—Martin H. Fischer

292

An important part of learning is to keep an open mind—something worthwhile may drop into it.

I have never let my schooling interfere with my education.

—Mark Twain

Example is the school of mankind, and they will learn at no other.

—Edmund Burke

The art of pleasing consists in being pleased.

—William Hazlitt

When things are
steep, remember to
stay level-headed.

—Horace

It is easy to be
wise after the event.

-Proverb

The readiness is all.

-William Shakespeare

It is good to know what a man is, and also what the world takes him for. But you do not understand him until you have learnt how he understands himself.

—F. H. Bradley

Self-reflection is the school of wisdom.

—Baltasar Gracian

Have a heart that never hardens, and a temper that never fires, and a touch that never hurts.

—Charles Dickens

The person who believes he knows everything will be passed by those who know they don't.

Take things as
they come.

-Proverb

There are tones
of voice that mean more
than words.

-Robert Frost

your own gift can present every moment with the cumulative force of a whole life's cultivation.

—Ralph Waldo Emerson

Seeing the intellectual growth of one of your students take place before your very eyes makes some of the difficulties associated with teaching suddenly bearable.

In case of doubt, it is better to say too little than too much.

—Thomas Jefferson

I never lose an opportunity of urging a practical beginning, however small, for it is wonderful how often in such matters the mustard seed germinates and roots itself.

—Florence Nightingale

The universe is too
great a mystery for
there to be only one single
approach to it.

-Symmachus

What would life be
without arithmetic,
but a scene of horrors? **311**

-Rev. Sydney Smith

For all knowledge and wonder
(which is the seed of knowledge) is
an impression of pleasure in itself.

—Francis Bacon

The whole art of teaching is only the art of awakening the natural curiosity of young minds for the purpose of satisfying it afterwards.

—Anatole France

Not only is there but one way of doing things rightly, but there is only one way of seeing them, and that is, seeing the whole of them.

—John Ruskin

$\mathbf{S}$imple as it seems, it was a great discovery that the key of knowledge could turn both ways, that it could open, as well as lock, the door of power to the many.

—James Russell Lowell

A human being is not,
in any proper
sense, a human being
until he is educated.

-Horace Mann

We are born for
cooperation, as are
the feet, the
hands, the eyelids, and the 317
upper and lower jaws.

-Marcus Aurelius
Antoninus

Teachers may be underpaid and overworked, but so much more greatly appreciated are they by those who realize that they have learned something from them.

He alone is worthy of the Appellation who either does great things, or teaches how they may be done, or describes them with a suitable majesty when they have been done.

—John Milton

Nature gave men two ends—one to sit on and one to think with. Ever since then man's success or failure has been dependent on the one he used most.

—George R. Kirkpatrick

Iron rusts from disuse, stagnant water loses its purity, and in cold weather becomes frozen; even so does inaction sap the vigors of the mind.

—Leonardo da Vinci

Facts are stubborn things.

-Alain Rene Le Sage

To teach is to guide the learner to a place he or she has never seen.

Upon the subject of education, not presuming to dictate any plan or system respecting it, I can only say that I view it as the most important subject which we, as a people, can be engaged in.

—Abraham Lincoln

Thinking leads men to knowledge. One may see and hear and read and learn as much as he pleases; he will never know any of it except that which he has thought over, that which by thinking he has made the property of his mind. Is it then saying too much if I say that man by thinking only becomes truly great?

—Johann Heinrich Pestalozzi

I teach you the Superman. Man is something that is to be surpassed. What have you done to surpass him?

—Friedrich Nietzsche

To understand is hard.
Once one understands,
action is easy.

—Sun Yat-sen

Knowing the answer to a question is not as important as being able to find the answer.

Keep the golden mean between saying too much and too little.

-Publius Syrus

329

What a teacher doesn't say is a telling part of what a student hears.

—Maurice Natanson

A good teacher is one who helps you become who you feel yourself to be.

—Julius Lester

Teaching is selflessness in the service of others.

—Berlie J. Fallon

To teach something you don't know is like coming back from someplace you've never been.

—Anonymous

My joy in learning
is partly that it
enables me to teach.

-Seneca

One good teacher in a lifetime may sometimes change a delinquent into a solid citizen.

-Phillip Wylie

It is a reality that the word "earning" is a part of "learning."

Men exist for the sake of one another. Teach them then or bear with them.

—Marcus Aurelius Antoninus

Knowledge is proud that he has learned so much;
Wisdom is humble that he knows no more.

—William Cowper

Education is...hanging around until you've caught on.

—Robert Frost

Often, the only praise many young children receive is from teachers at school.

Be not afraid of growing slowly, be afraid only of standing still.

341

-Chinese proverb

Any subject can be taught effectively in some intellectually honest form to any child at any stage of development.

—Jerome Seymour Bruner

If we succeed in giving the love of learning, the learning itself is sure to follow.

—John Lubbock

Some books are to be tasted, others to be swallowed, and some few to be chewed and digested.

—Francis Bacon

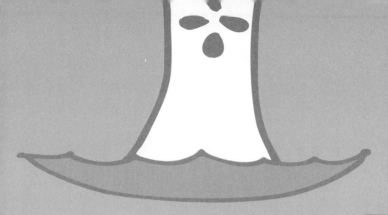

345

Never tell people how to do things. Tell them what to do and they will surprise you with their ingenuity.

—George S. Patton

If you have knowledge,
let others light their candles
at it.

-Margaret Fuller

346

Beware of the
man of one book.

-Isaac D'Israeli

The confidence which we have in ourselves gives birth to much of that which we have in others.

—François de La Rochefoucauld

Curiosity is one of the permanent and certain characteristics of a vigorous intellect.

—Samuel Johnson

The things taught in schools and colleges are not an education, but the means of education.

—Ralph Waldo Emerson

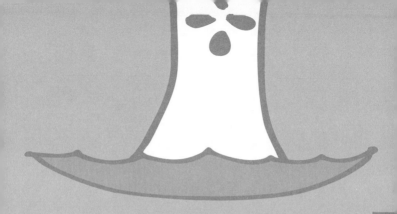

Is there anyone so
wise as to learn by the
experience of others?

—Francois Voltaire

Every fact that is learned becomes a key to other facts.

-E. L. Youmans

Delight in teaching
what you have learned.

353

-Seneca

Education does not mean teaching people what they do not know...It is a painful, continual, and difficult work to be done by kindness, by watching, by warning, by precept, and by praise, but above all—by example.

—John Ruskin

Education does not take place
in a vacuum. It takes a village to
educate a child.

An idea, to be suggestive, must come to the individual with the force of a revelation.

—William James

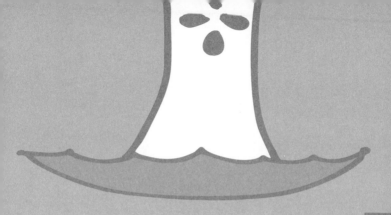

357

It is necessary to try to surpass one's self always; this occupation ought to last as long as life.

—Queen Christina

He who has
imagination without learning
has wings but no feet.

-Joseph Joubert

Instinct is untaught ability.

-Alexander Bain

How many young geniuses we have known.

-Ralph Waldo Emerson

It takes all sorts to make a world.

—English proverb

The word impossible is not in
my dictionary.

—Napoleon Bonaparte

Style, in writing or speaking, is formed very early in life, while the imagination is warm and impressions are permanent.

—Thomas Jefferson

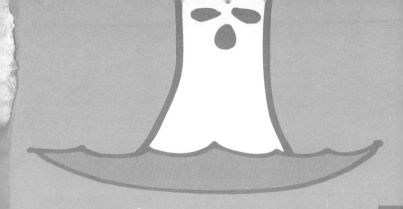

What greater or better
gift can we offer the
republic than to teach our
youth?

—Marcus Tullius Cicero

364

365

The immense
amount of
knowledge in any
discipline is created
one small bit at a time.